And Then There Was Light

Stories, Poems, and Devotionals

Vol. 1

Carolina Christian Writers' Conference

Compiled by
Living Parables of Central Florida

And Then There Was Light

Stories, Poems, and Devotionals

Vol. 1

Carolina Christian Writers' Conference

Copyright © 2021 Living Parables of Central Florida, Inc.

All rights reserved.

ISBN: 978-1-952369-86-5

Cover Illustration: Dave O'Connell
Cover Design: Bob Ousnamer

Published by EA Books Publishing a division of
Living Parables of Central Florida, Inc. a 501c3
EABooksPublishing.com

ACKNOWLEDGMENTS

We'd like to thank the director of this conference—Linda Gilden—for encouraging and equipping writers for the glory of the Kingdom of God. We wish to thank Cheri Cowell and her wonderful team at EABooks Publishing for giving us this opportunity. We thank our many friends and family for supporting us in our writing dreams. And most importantly, we want to thank our Lord and Savior Jesus Christ for His gifts—may this book bring You the honor and glory You deserve.

TABLE OF CONTENTS

Acknowledgments	iii

Carolina Christian Writers Conference

Who Am I? *Paul Shotsberger*	1
Rooted in Faith *Amber McKinney Collins*	3
When God's Plan Doesn't Match Our Dreams *Becky Antkowiak*	7
Fill Your Heart With Love *C. K. Sharpe*	13
Strikes A-Hoy *Kay K. Mortimer*	17
Prophecies, Prayer, and Momma *Kenneth Perkins*	21
Alone *Christina Sinisi*	27
A New Day *Glenda Durano*	33
Saul's Darkness *Rhonnie Cough*	37
Night Light *L. A. Robbins*	39

Dark Knight   44
Sandra Vosburgh

Having Faith with Chronic Illness   47
Taryn Dryfhout

Sally and Buster   51
Cheryl D. Coffman

The Light Diffuses   56
Melody M. Morrison

One More Little One   59
Adria Wilkins

Tears at a Church Meeting   62
Melissa Henderson

True Light Shines   65
Tammy Hill

INTRODUCTION

When dark turns to light, weakness turns to strength, despair to hope, and death to life—there is a story. The Greatest Story Ever Told begins this way and our stories are a part of this grand story. We invite you to join us for a journey into our darkness and learn how God used those dark places to transform us, our lives, and the lives of those around us. Through poems, prayers, devotions, and stories you will catch a glimpse of the Light that shatters the deepest darkness. Because in the darkest of nights, God is— and then there was light.

Carolina Christian Writers Conference

Who Am I?

Paul Shotsberger

Who am I? I'm a walking contradiction. I care about people, but sometimes I think so much about myself that I that I don't notice hurting people around me, even my friends. I say good words and think good thoughts in church, and then I go live my life the way I want to the rest of the week. I'm so easily wounded by what people say, but, my goodness, how the hurtful words fly out of my mouth sometimes.

Who am I? I'm a pretty responsible person, but that's not who I am, even though that's the way a lot of people think of me. People want me to be so many things—it's all so complicated. They want me to be things and do things that just aren't in me. I try my best to please people, but there's only so much of me to go around. Most days I'm more aware of my limitations than anything else.

Who am I? Well, I'm not the healthiest person in the world. It's funny, people look at me and because I look normal on the outside, they assume I'm normal on the inside too. But I've got some things wrong with me, and some days are really hard. And in case you're wondering, no, I'm not just talking about physical problems—there are other things too, the things nobody talks about but everybody understands.

Who am I? I'm a sinner, but Jesus died on the cross just for me. And He's getting a mansion ready for me. And He cares about my hopes and dreams—in fact, He put them in me. He's put the light of eternity in my heart and asked me to shine it everywhere I go. I can make a difference in this world because His divine power has given me everything I need for life and godliness.

Who am I? I am you.

Dr. Paul Shotsberger is Professor of Graduate Faculty at Southern Wesleyan University. Prior to his current position, he served as an officer in the United States Navy, a high school mathematics teacher, and a missionary to Ukraine. He lives in Seneca, South Carolina with his wife of forty-one years.

Rooted in Faith

Amber McKinney Collins

"Those who sow in tears will reap with songs of joy. He who goes out weeping, carrying the seed to sow, will return with songs of joy, carrying sheaves with him."

Psalm 126: 5-6 (NIV)

Gardening was something I always said I wanted to try, but with past endeavors, I quickly learned I had a black thumb. When the pandemic hit, everyone on social media was talking about learning a new skill, while they were out of work and quarantining at home. I thought, "Well here is my real chance, let's garden!" I have farmers in my family and I wanted to try out the family skill. I took some of the dark soil and placed it in the cup, I then gently laid the tomato seed on top and proceeded to bury the seed with more soil. I watered the seed, fertilized the dirt, and even sang to the little seed, but nothing happened. Weeks went by and I was following all the rules, from the various websites rendered from the "How to Grow the Perfect Tomato" search, but still nothing. I thought, "Well there it is, my black thumb, forever destined to shop for fresh veggies at the farmers market and local produce stands; never to have my own garden." I was disappointed and saddened, but determined to get this tiny tomato plant to grow. I followed all the "tricks," I measured the water, watered at the right time of day, gave the appropriate amount of sunlight. I sang to the plant, every time I watered, and I prayed over that little seed. A few more weeks went by, and one morning I saw it, the teeny tiny little sprig of green. I shouted for joy and praised God I had a tiny plant! Maybe I didn't have a black thumb after all. In my moment of joy, I couldn't help but think about the verse in Psalm 126: 5b (NIV), *"Those… will reap with songs of joy."* There was my joy. I finally had a tomato plant. As I studied God's word, He spoke to me through the joy of that tiny tomato plant.

During this time in my life, I was in a season overwhelmed with sadness and I, myself, felt like I was being buried and I wondered if I would even sprout forth again with new sprigs of life. That's why I tried gardening, good for the soul, body and mind. I felt dead, much like I thought that little seed was. The watering and fertilizing of that little seed eventually represented the Word of God I was pouring over daily. The Word was my own water and fertilizer as I looked for answers to all my "why" questions. The singing to that little seed represented the praise and worship music I belted daily, even when I didn't feel like praising God. Many days the tears of sorrow and hurt were more prevalent than shouts of joy. However, the moment when the green leaf poked through the dark soil, God showed me a moment of joy, a moment of light in the darkness. Even though I felt buried, God's word was nurturing and it was taking care of me, so I too could sprout up from the darkness. Isaiah 43:19 (NIV) says, *"For I am about to do something new. See I have already begun! Do you not see it?"* Honestly, no I didn't see it, until I saw that little seed bring forth new life and I realized God is doing the same for me. When God planted me in a season of sorrow, I knew one day, I too, would bloom into something more beautiful, according to His purpose.

Do you feel buried today? Well, don't fret! Stay in the Word, keep listening to the praise and worship music, and I promise, you too will bloom. Your old story will pass away to a new and even more glorious story. We then can go forth with our songs of joy and tell others what God has done for us!

Father God,

Thank you that you know exactly what we need when we need it! Thank you that you are the water for our thirsty soul, the bread of life and you make all things new. You may have to plant us deep in the soil, so we can bloom and share your good news with the world! Help me see my circumstances through your eyes and remember that your will and plan for my life is always better than the one I create. Thank you that you are in control! I love you!

In Jesus name,
Amen

Amber is a Christian introvert, who prefers to share her story through written word. She loves to travel and uses nature as her inspiration to write and paint. She is an elementary school teacher, wife, and mother to several "fur babies." She loves music, painting, reading and writing.

When God's Plan Doesn't Match Our Dreams

Becky Antkowiak

Strands of "what I'll be when I grow up" stitch through our childhoods. Early adult decisions about education, work, and family weave our wishes into tangible reality. As we age, grand ideas of legacy loom large.

We dream of making our mark.

And of course, no one dreams of loss of connection, of stability, of routine, or of family. But at some point, we all experience loss.

God is Bigger Than Our Depression

Loss brings sadness. Unchecked, sadness may spiral into depression.

Depression sucks us in like quicksand and drags us into despair. Our dreams and plans bring us hope.

We make plans to thrive, but we all know how quickly life can derail those plans. Unexpected delays, trials, illness, and even death interrupt our dreams.

In our most desperate times, we search God's Word for comforting verses such as, *"'I know the plans that I have for you,' declares the LORD, 'plans for prosperity and not for disaster, to give you a future and a hope'"* (Jeremiah 29:11, NASB). And we wonder how our current reality could possibly be a part of God's plan.

I'm not suggesting God causes depression, but He may use difficult circumstances to turn our hearts back to Him.

As individuals, as families, as a country—we're comfortable, surrounded by shiny or big or expensive toys. Diversions.

In the Bible, when God wanted someone's attention, they ended up in the desert. We hear God's voice more clearly when distractions disappear.

Most of my distractions—and my ability to connect with people—disappeared when quarantine and social distancing began. I joke about being a serial extrovert, but my need for relationships is real. In fewer than sixty days, I fractured.

As my dreams disintegrated, God waited for me to turn to Him. God loves to heal our broken hearts and lives. He's the master of turning ashes into a phoenix.

God is Bigger Than Our Needs

We have needs. Need for food. Need for shelter. Need for work. Need for connection.

However, our greatest need is true stability. True family. True love. Most of all, we need a connection to God. Too often, we forget that connection.

Imagine: you open your email to find a message from a foreign prince, informing you that his father, a quadribillionaire, has decided to adopt you. If you accept the adoption, you are welcome to move into the palace and you will someday inherit half the estate. Anytime you need something, just contact the prince and he'll make arrangements.

Let's say you accept the offer, after checking with a lawyer to confirm the email is legitimate. Your perspective on life will likely change. *Urgent needs? No sweat. My new dad will provide.*

Philippians 4:19 says, *"God will supply all your needs according to His riches in glory in Christ Jesus"* (NASB).

I'm not preaching some kind of prosperity gospel. Christians suffer just like anyone else. But our perspective is different because we know the answer to "who's your Daddy?" If we have a relationship with Jesus, our future is secure. Even when we have a temporal, physical need, our need for spiritual stability isn't in jeopardy. And often, God does provide for our physical needs in miraculous ways.

After a few months of social distancing, I didn't recognize God's riches. I didn't grasp the goodness of what He was working to create. Instead of embracing the ability to nurture a few special relationships, I grumbled. Rather than focusing on the many blessings, I mourned my inability to regain what I wanted most: a life full of personal connections.

We think we know what we want—fame, success, money. Hugs and face-to-face conversation. But we'll always have a driving desire for more. Can you imagine an individual with fame, success or money turning down the opportunity to double their share? Would you? Would I?

God offers us a bigger *more*. God proposes *"immeasurably more than all we can ask or imagine"* (Ephesians 3:20 NIV), but sometimes He first asks us to let go of our dreams.

When we fight for the good future we think we want, it can interfere with the better future God imagines for us. Some of God's dreams for us involve preparation and education.

Thanks to online school, some of us experienced a living metaphor of God's interactions with us. We know an education is in our children's best interest. Our children would much rather play online games. With our children's future success in mind, we created environments in which our children had no choice but to learn, even when our sweaty, kicking, screaming kiddos didn't see the point.

I hoped social distancing would just go away. I prayed God would resolve the situation so I could attend a favorite conference. Instead, I had to cancel my ticket and settle for virtual attendance. While God wove strands to create the beautiful tapestry He planned, I flopped into a tantrum of my own, railing at the unfairness.

We may not find God's training and education enjoyable, but He knows what we're going to need for future success. And He knows that His dreams for us are immeasurably more incredible than the ones we imagine ourselves.

God is Bigger Than Our Buts

But I'm tired.
But I want to turn off my brain and binge-watch a series.
But I'm not an expert.
But I don't have the talent.
But I might offend someone.
But I'm angry my reality looks different from my expectation.

Give us time, and we can come up with a big *but* for any situation.

Grumbling about the isolation of my new reality, I clicked a random chapter in my audio Bible. I found myself in Exodus, listening to the familiar story of God's plan to rescue his people from slavery.

As Moses approached the burning bush, my thoughts wandered, and God nudged me to create an opportunity for connection. Maybe virtual interaction during the conference. Perhaps an online group for other writers feeling isolated.

But my IT friends joke about my lack of technological ability, and the conference leadership might say no. But even if I create a group of my own, no one will join. But what if I can't stick with it? But…but…but…

My attention returned to Exodus just when Moses argued with God about his speaking ability. I rolled my eyes. Wow. God speaks directly to Moses, and he argues. What an idio—oh. Right.

People have been arguing with God for centuries. Millenia. We say "but" because we're scared. He's bigger than all our buts, and if we let go (which is harder than it sounds) He'll smash those fears.

God is Bigger, but He's Not a Bully

God is bigger than our fears, bigger than our circumstances, bigger than our feelings. He's big enough to pull us out of the mire. Big enough to save us. Big enough to love us. Big enough to let us choose whether we'll follow Him.

If God calls us, He will prepare us, if we'll stop making excuses. He's promised to give us His power to get things done, if we'll let Him. He can—and will—love anyone and everyone through us, if we'll just stop backpedaling. God will provide everything we need to work His plan and attain His dream for our lives, if we'll quit arguing with Him.

God is willing to direct our steps, provide for our needs, use us despite our flaws, and take us further than we can dream. To reach that place, we must commit to listening—to *hearing*—His voice, to eliminating excuses, and to following His plan, even if it doesn't line up with what we think we want to do.

And when God's plans don't line up with our expectations, we have to trust Him enough not to take back control. If we allow our human control-freak nature to take over, He'll wait until we're ready—but we might miss a cool opportunity to watch His plans take shape if we hang onto our control too long. Relinquishing control of our dreams makes room for God's plans.

God can use a life circumstance we would never choose for ourselves to create ministry opportunities we might never imagine. He can help us overcome fears and accomplish what we consider impossible. I know, because He did this for me. His plans for us are bigger than anything we can conceive. When God's plans don't match our dreams, we just have to trust Him.

Becky Antkowiak is a writer, speaker, editor, adoptive homeschooling mom, Compassion sponsor, and enthusiastic Grammar Floozy. Becky believes every stranger is a friend she hasn't met. She founded the 540 Club, a free group for writers focused on encouraging each other in the writing journey. Connect with Becky at 540Club.org.

Fill Your Heart With Love

C. K. Sharpe

Sitting transfixed in front of the family's black and white television, I watched four mop-heads singing for the first time live in the United States. Their songs encapsulated love and the need for it. The Beatles' appearance on the Ed Sullivan Show, February 9, 1964, was broadcast live from Studio 50 in NYC. It is etched in my mind as distinct as the United States' 35th Presidential assassination of John F. Kennedy almost two years prior on November 22, 1963.

Anyway, I thought the Brits had something to be proud of as I sat cross-legged in front of the television watching the longhaired musicians in '64. The Beatles' over-the-top music arrangements and simple lyrics rang out in our living room, across continents, and changed the world; or at least, the music industry.

It is probably safe to say there might be a few post-war teens, that don't remember the sixties, but most do. The simple lyrics of love songs written in that era became life-model aspirations for many 20th-century youth. Some thought the mop-top musicians were ahead of their time. I believe they weren't. They were just in time to claim their part in changing a confused culture.

In America, "Beatlemania" impinged on restless youth trapped by the uncertainties of the Vietnam Conflict. As far as I was concerned, the movie "Good Morning, Vietnam," that came out much later in '87, was the only good thing that came out of a disturbing era.

Jesus didn't start his ministry carrying sheet music and a guitar, although people sang and cried for joy at his words. He didn't have a T.V. broadcast, podcast, or blog to promote His message of love—no cell phones either. He had His Father in Heaven, twelve great friends, and the backing of Angels. His message was simple. Through faith, God offers His love to humanity through salvation and the gift of eternal life.

Jesus put deliverance from sin on the map; albeit the earth. He not only preached the Good News—believe in Him and love others—through His words, but also powerfully showed the Good News through His actions. How did He get it so right—through love, that's how. Jesus' self-sacrificing love communicated deep feelings for us. Through His sacrifice, we have been given a fantastic knowledge of God's enduring presence in our lives—now that is true love. His simple message was clear and straightforward. It is everlasting and is still heard across continents. His Word changes worldviews

The mop-top musicians back in the day recognized and sang about the need for love in the world.

That need is still as apropos as it was over two thousand years ago. We need love and Jesus' love is easy to find. Simply open His Word in faith and seek Him. Pray to Him. He will fill your heart with His love. In His love, we can walk in the light, and enjoy living daily in His presence.

Who could want anything more than given the gift of love; an eternal light that lives in the heart?

Today's Scripture: *"But if we walk in the light, as he is in the light, we have fellowship with one another, and the blood of Jesus, his Son, purifies us from all sin."* (1 John 1:7 NIV).

Cheryl Sharpe is a bold proclaimer of the word. Her writing declares Bible Truths that show the power of God's love and forgiveness. Her devotions are always relevant and on target. She has written two 40-day Devotionals, *Miracles of Jesus* and its companion Bible Study, and *Fix My Heart*.

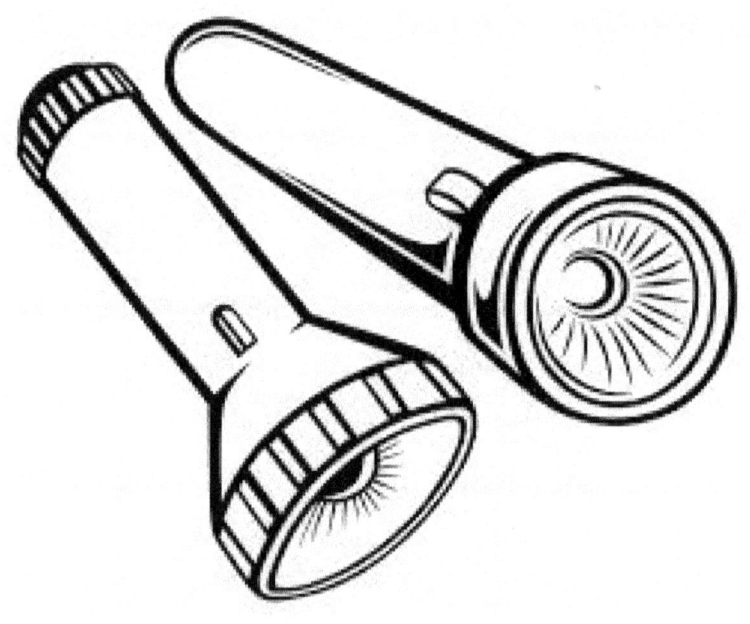

Strikes A-Hoy

Kay K. Mortimer

The pitcher throws the ball. The batter hits a drive down the right field line, scooped up by an outfielder. The third-base runner charges and slides into home plate, just as the throw comes into the catcher. Safe or out? We wait for the umpire's signal.

The umpire waves both hands back and forth: safe. But where did the umpire learn the signals to use? The answer lies over one hundred years ago in the contributions of one special player.

In 1886, twenty-four-year-old William Ellsworth Hoy began his professional baseball career. Born in Ohio during the Civil War, William Hoy loved baseball, and He learned to play as a child, despite a severe handicap: permanent deafness due to meningitis. In spite of his disability, he became an outstanding player.

Hoy's illustrious career began in Oshkosh, Wisconsin. He soon played Major League Baseball for the Washington Senators, the Cincinnati Reds, and other teams. His teammates nicknamed him "Dummy" because he was deaf.

Imagine Hoy's disadvantage. The umpires shouted out the calls of "safe," "out," "ball," or "strike." Unable to hear, he didn't know what call the umpire gave. How could he overcome this obstacle?

Hoy began by asking the umpires to raise their right arm for a strike and left arm for a ball. He also created signs for "safe" and "out," adapted from American Sign Language.

Umpires began using the signs for all games, and still use them today.

William Hoy not only received from the sport of baseball but also gave much to it, holding a remarkable record. An outstanding outfielder, he threw out three men at home plate from the outfield in one game in 1889, only one of few men in history to accomplish this feat. In his rookie year, he led the National League with eighty-two stolen bases. To his credit, he was also a great lead-off hitter and one of the fastest base runners in the sport's history. He hit the second grand slam of the newly-established American League in 1901. In 1902, batting for the Cincinnati Reds, he faced a deaf pitcher, named Luther Haden Taylor. "It was the only time in major league history that two deaf players faced each other."[1]

Mac Davis' quote, from *100 Greatest Baseball Heroes*, 1974, said, *"In his brilliant fourteen-year big-league career, the 'Amazing Dummy' played in 1,784 games, hit 236 doubles, 118 triples, and 41 homers, to finish with a lifetime total of 2,057 safe hits. He also scored 1,419 runs, and stole 605 bases."*[2] Hoy was quite an amazing player, especially considering that he could neither speak nor hear.

After Hoy left professional baseball in 1902, he didn't leave the sport. He later became a personnel director for several hundred deaf employees at Goodyear and coached a deaf baseball club from 1919 to 1920. In October of 1961, ninety-nine-year-old Hoy threw the ceremonial first pitch in Game Three of the World Series between the Cincinnati Reds and the New York Yankees. Two months later, just <u>short of one hundred years</u> old, he died of a stroke.

[1] "A Brief Overview of Hoy's Career." https://www.dummyhoy.com/overview/#:~:text=On%20May%2016%2C%201902%2C%20%E2%80%9C,deaf%20players%20faced%20each%20other. Accessed May 5, 2020.

[2] "What They Said: Hall of Famers on Hoy (and other quotes)." https://www.dummyhoy.com/what_they_said/ Accessed May 5, 2020

Hoy also exemplified excellent character and sportsmanship. He maintained legendary honesty, rarely being thrown out of a game. The story is told that, during one game as dusk fell, the umpire called the batter out when a ball was seemingly caught by the centerfielder. The umpire asked Hoy, who was the centerfielder, if it was caught on the bounce or on the fly. Honest Hoy told him it was "caught 'on the bounce'. The umpire called the batter safe. Hoy's teammates were furious. Hoy was satisfied that he had told the truth."[3] Even his character exuded integrity, making him an example for other players.

Since 2001, Hoy has been an inductee into the Cincinnati Reds' Hall of Fame and the Ohio Baseball Hall of Fame. There have been many attempts to induct him into the National Baseball Hall of Fame, but without success to date. Although rarely known by baseball fans, many credit him with leaving a huge impact on the game.

The sport of baseball owes William Hoy a great debt. Old newspapers as far back as 1888 refer to Hoy's contributions of establishing the hand signals that still speak loud and clear today. On April 8, 2001, Gallaudet University dedicated its on-campus baseball field to William "Dummy" Hoy, "a player they called an inspiration and role model for the deaf community."[4]

The next time we watch the umpire's signals at a baseball game, we can remember the impact of one man on the entire sport. His name is William Ellsworth Hoy, not "Dummy" Hoy.

Hoy's abilities far outweighed any disabilities he had, and the sport of baseball is forever grateful for this man and his gifts. Joshua Evans, in the July 26, 1991 issue of Sports

---

[3] "A Capsule Biography." http://www.dummyhoy.com/overview/bio.html. Accessed May 5, 2020.

[4] "Gallaudet Dedicates Diamon." https://www.dummyhoy.com/news_update/ Accessed May 5, 2020.

Collectors Digest, said, *"He is a symbol of people who just need to be given a chance — a chance to be treated just like everyone else."*[5]

In baseball history, one man illuminated this family favorite pastime. One person did make a difference. Although he died many years ago, his contribution to the sport of baseball lives on, making everyone's enjoyment of the game even better because of it. And he shines as an example of the light one individual can share to bless the lives of so many.

Kay Mortimer teaches and writes from a heart of passion for the Word of God, encouraging others with her words. Her articles, broadcasts, and books can best be found by visiting her website: www.covenanttruthministries.com, as her passion for her Lord drives her daily to pursue His messages.

---

[5] "What They Said: Hall of Famers on Hoy (and other quotes)." https://www.dummyhoy.com/what_they_said/ Accessed May 5, 2020.

Prophecies, Prayer, and Momma

Kenneth Perkins

Waking up to death is rarely a good thing. On the morning of July 17, 1944, while getting dressed for the day, Rena Woods Bell had been told of a scuffle that occurred the night before. Something involving her cousin, another man, another woman. Guns were drawn. Shots fired. Bodies dropped. Having awakened from the dream, she simply figured it was about the scuffle and perhaps an overactive imagination. Then the thought came to her: was it her cousin who died? God Forbid.

But it was neither.

Her son, Silas, had awakened that morning 1,100 miles away in a small apartment in Northern California feeling just as edgy. Not from dreams or night sweats as she had, but an overwhelming feeling of dread from what the day might bring. He knew what he was to do that morning before he left for work and he did as the Spirit instructed him.

That day he was scheduled for a late shift at a Naval munitions depot in Port Chicago, a heavy-eyed, one stoplight town some 30 miles north of San Francisco. Port Chicago was constructed in the early 1940s for a specific purpose: keep up with the high demand for weaponry to supply World War II troops.

A base at nearby Mare Island was unable to satisfy the weapon count. Mare Island averaged moving 8.7 tons per hatch per hour so the laborers at Port Chicago, where Silas worked, were given a target goal of redeploying 10 tens per hatch per hour. Silas' job was to transfer bullets, depth charges, artillery shells and 1,000- to 2,000-pound bombs from train cars into the holds of waiting ships docked at the main pier. The work was grueling, and as was the case for the military's menial labor in this era of brutal segregation, it fell mostly on the shoulders of Black sailors like him. The 125-man crews slogged away on shifts that never stopped. The emphasis was speed above all else. Silas and the other soldiers were rewarded for keeping up or punished for falling behind.

He despised the work. He told his family that he felt it was dangerous because they hadn't really been trained in this sort of thing, particularly the handling of high explosives and munitions. The dull, assembly-line type work left a gapping margin of error for workers whose repetitive and robotic movement gave them a false sense of security. It became almost comatose-like work, akin to what one might experience on a mind-numbing cross-country drive on a dark road.

By about 10 p.m. that night, Silas and other sailors were looking forward to heading home after having packed the hold of the 440-foot *E.A. Bryan* with nearly 5,000 tons of high explosives and ammunition. They were tired, hungry, and frustrated.

Then something happened.

Shortly after 10:18 p.m., nearly everyone in Port Chicago heard an earsplitting boom followed by a blinding burst of flames. A second, larger blast came about six seconds later and sent scorched metal shooting into an otherwise clear, night sky. The *E.A. Bryan*, with Silas still inside, and a nearby locomotive were entirely incinerated, and the second ship was tossed some 500 feet away, landing in pieces, as though it were a toy boat. The blast was so massive a number of buildings in Port Chicago crumbled. Windows as far away as San Francisco rattled or were completely blown out. If this were an earthquake, it would have registered a 3.4 on the Richter scale, seismologists at the time reported.

The 320 men working on the ships perished instantly; those on the pier were killed as well, and several hundred more in the area were injured or maimed by shattered debris. The exact cause of the explosion was never uncovered although blame was placed on Black sailors for their "mishandling" of explosives.

Silas' wife was at the apartment during the blast, which blew out most of the apartment windows. Glass scattered across the dining room table, the living room couch, the bathroom, and her infant's crib.

Silas' 17-year-old baby sister, Macie Bell, was at Silas' Fort Worth home that evening visiting from East Texas. It was her favorite place to be. She loved "the big city," loved her big brother, even though he was, like their mother, a bit overprotective at times. Couldn't do this - couldn't do that. But that's why she was allowed to go there in the first place. Her mother, Rena, was a strict disciplinarian who wanted nothing less from anyone who was going to be overseeing her baby girl.

When I spoke with Macie she told me her mother couldn't read nor write, didn't have any kind of formal education but "she knew Scripture through and through. When we were growing up, she would pick up the Bible and could recite it word for word," she said. "My cousins thought she was reading it. She memorized it from what my daddy had told her."

When her mother died, Macie, still heartbroken over her brother's death, explained how she was there at her bedside. She remembers the slowness of her breath, the blinking of her eyes. At one point Rena Woods Bell sat up, opened her eyes, and shook her head no. Then no again. Then yes.

Then she laid her head on the pillow.

And died.

Macie said, "For a long time I wondered who was talking to my mother—someone was—and what they were saying, but I do know that my dreams after that became more clear, as if God was talking to me just like he talked to her."

Over the years Macie, now 94, had her own prophetic dreams, about her own siblings, all of who have passed on before her, as well as dreams about her own children, some of whom have also passed.

"People who weren't believers would think my mother was weird or crazy for having prophetic dreams," she said. "So they must think I'm weird and crazy, too. In the Bible, God talks about revealing himself in visions and speaking to us in dreams. I haven't any visions like that, but I have had dreams. So if the Bible talks about God speaking to you in dreams, then it's God talking to you. You might be asleep in the natural world, but your heart stays awake in the spiritual world. That means He continues to meet with us at night because it's the only time our minds are quiet enough to hear what He has to say. We need to shut up to listen sometimes."

She always said the first question to ask about dreams is whether it's from God. You know it is if it's close to Scripture but if it goes against the Word or the nature of God, it comes from another place.

"Before Jesus went to heaven He told his disciples He was sending someone to help them," Macie said. "That was His promise and God never breaks His promises. When you believe in Christ, the Holy Spirit immediately becomes part of you. It's permanent. He leads us in the way we should go and reveals God's truths. So the Holy Spirit was telling my brother what was about to happen. Not exactly how and when but that he was not coming back. So He told him what to tell his wife and to say goodbye to his babies. He knew he wasn't coming back and he didn't. Even today he is still listed as missing in action. They never found an actual body."

After her mother's death, Macie had dreams about Silas almost constantly. In every one, her brother was taking his family to church.

"I would see him walk up the steps and into the church door," Macie said. "God wanted me to know he was saved. He was in his early 40s. He was so young. But I knew he was with Jesus because that's exactly what God told me."

"From that point, it lifted me up. It gave me a sense of peace. After so many years of feeling lost and bitter and angry about what happened, there was peace, and I knew why."

Now she has a better idea of her mother's deathbed conversation.

"To guide me, to help me find myself, to pull me out of my darkness, to help others through my own dreams, to see life in a different way," Macie said. "That's the conversation He had with her about me. Now I pray I have that same conversation with my daughter. And my daughter has that conversation with *her* daughter."

Kenneth Perkins is a Fort Worth, Texas-based journalist who has written for major market newspapers such as the Chicago Tribune and Dallas Morning News. He is currently a full-time freelance writer whose work appears in various magazines, newspapers and online publications.

Alone

Christina Sinisi

Barbara closed the front door and walked back into the living room. The formal room had been rarely used when the house was overrun with a husband, growing boys and a Labradoodle. Now, it was her first line of retreat. Maybe because her arthritis acted up more than it acted down, and the couch closest to the front door was the tufted monstrosity they'd inherited from Jim's parents.

Another connection to people long gone. Jim's parents had died a decade ago, his father of a heart attack and her second mother of a broken heart. The painting of sunflowers had been a Christmas gift from her long-gone older sister — who smoked all her life even though she'd known what she was doing to herself.

Not all deaths made sense. Her husband had been healthier than she'd ever been. Jim played hockey and went to the gym. Up until the day a heart attack claimed him like a ticket punched by the great conductor, he'd challenged her to keep up with his get up and go. Then, he was gone.

Her right knee crackled like lightning, not that she claimed her disability portended rain. She just hurt.

The couch pillow poked the small of her back and needed re-adjusting. In a few minutes, once she got over her son's leaving, she might head into the kitchen. Afternoon tea was a lasting tradition from her English grandmother, so long gone that Barbara had trouble picturing her.

Without thinking, maybe because it was another established habit, her fingers fumbled with the latch to the end table drawer. On top perched the photo album her daughter-in-law Laurie had made her. Barbara's only son, Brad, was a police officer, and Laurie filled her every loose minute with trying not to worry. The woman was thirty years younger than Barbara, but she passed for her sister when they went out.

The album held photos of everyone Barbara had ever loved—-her grandparents, parents, and sisters. Laurie hadn't stopped with the dead, though. There was also Brad, standing tall and proud in his uniform. He and Laurie hadn't been able to have children of their own. They had gone through the treatments, but it just hadn't happened. Ten years ago, they'd completed all the paperwork and saved up the money. But, Laurie, an only child who did all the yard work around the house and worked more hours than her husband, got cold feet.

The adoption never happened and Barbara didn't have grandchildren.

Glancing around the room, her gaze touched upon the other objects in the drawer. This had been Jim's spot in the morning, in his later years. He'd always been a believer, but somehow it had gotten more serious with old age in the hallway. His Bible was there, the one with his underlines and his notepad. She'd read every word on those pages over the last five years. There was no comfort in them anymore since she'd memorized every syllable. The Bible might offer comfort, but her anger at God simmered and steamed and blurred the words.

The other object was cold and metal and never offered comfort to anyone—an absence of pain, maybe, but never comfort. Jim had kept it with him at all times, to protect her he said. Jim hadn't been able to protect her from his own dying and this blanket of loneliness she tucked around her shoulders and walked around the house with to combat the cold.

"Speaking of which," she said to no one and pushed to stand. She had no trouble with worrying about whether she was going crazy since most of the time no one was around to judge. "I can put the heat up now that boy has left. Complaining about suffocating from the heat, as if I don't know I'm old and my body don't regulate temperature as good as it used to."

Shuffling, taking her time adjusting from the fancy living room rug to the hardwood in the foyer, Barbara stared at the thermostat. She lived alone. She was financially stable, Jim having provided for her real well. She could set the thing on 80 degrees if she wanted. So she did.

The kitchen shone bright in the late afternoon sun, white cabinets and pale gray walls reflecting the light bouncing off the pool. Echoes of little boy splashes and manly cannonballs had her leaning against the granite countertop, fighting for breath.

"You're not weak, Barbara. You never have been." She hadn't been. Her parents had been dirt poor farmers in the Upstate and she'd worked as a secretary for forty-some years, while raising her son and watching over her sister's children when she died.

Her breath evened out and she grabbed the remote. One good thing about being by yourself, no one was around to hide the remote on you. The television flickered to life.

The news used to be depressing and to be avoided at all costs. Now, she liked the fact that the shows were broadcast live and not recorded. This way, she knew there were other people on the planet at this moment, living and breathing. The local and the national news passed by in a blur.

The calendar pages on the refrigerator ruffled with the rush of the air from the vent. Maybe she shouldn't have put the system on high. It felt like air from a volcano circulating.

Next Saturday was highlighted circled. She and Audine were to have gone shopping, only Audine had fallen or suffered from a stroke, no one could say which came first.

It would be comical if it wasn't death.

So many losses it didn't seem possible or real.

People would think she was making it up.

The newscaster's voice penetrated her awareness. "All people over 65 are urged to self-quarantine. It may take months for a vaccine."

The phone rang. Barbara answered. "Mom." Laurie cried on the other end. "There's been an accident. Brad."

Barbara listened, and then made her way back into the living room without making herself anything to eat. In that end table, there was comfort.

She fell rather than sat on the couch, the pillows still warm from her own body heat of minutes and a lifetime earlier. Her hand shook as if she had Parkinson's, one of the few diseases of old age she didn't have. She reopened the drawer and took out the photo album that had been her focus before. Now, she dropped the book of loving memories on the floor. Some small piece of sanity kept her from throwing it with all her pitiful might.

"God." She glanced at the Bible contemptuously. "What good are you, I ask you? What good does it do to believe in some great, all-powerful being who does things like this? My boy, my beautiful boy."

Her daughter-in-law's words echoed in her brain like the chimes fighting the wind on her back porch: uneasy, discordant with no rhyme or reason. "Mom. He was downtown. They didn't expect trouble. It's Charleston, everyone is always so nice."

But there had been a riot, on King Street and her beautiful boy—no, the fine upstanding man her son had become—tried to stop a mob from beating a man outside a bicycle shop. The mob had turned on him. Why had her Laurie called it an accident?

"Oh, then he'd been hit by a stray brick in the head." Laurie sounded numb.

He was in the hospital with a brain injury.

The doctors didn't know whether he'd live.

A mother should never outlive her child, never.

Barbara touched the gun. The metal was ice cold and hard.

"No."

Barbara jumped as if somebody poked her with a pin.

"What? Who?" She looked around the room, her head twisting around. Being alone was so much a part of her that she couldn't start to come up with an explanation.

Her hand reached for the weapon again, as if the body part had a mind of its own.

"No, my daughter. No."

Barbara felt the wrinkles on her face stretch as her eyes widened. A shaft of light came through the front picture window. Headlights.

"God?" Her voice cracked and the tears started. "Is that you?"

"Take and read."

She picked up the worn ESV Bible and rifled the pages, stopping at a passage her Jim had underlined twice. "John 12:35-36: *"The light is among you for a little while longer. Walk while you have the light, lest darkness overtake you. The one who walks in the darkness does not know where he is going. While you have the light, believe in the light, that you may become sons of light."*

The doorbell rang. Barbara swiped at the tears on her cheeks, and she pushed the gun away. The only light in the room came from the headlights outside that hadn't disappeared. She stood and walked in the light as she made her way to the front door.

"Who is it?"

"Mom, it's me, Laurie. Please let me in. Something told me to come get you. I need you, Mom. Please."

A member of ACFW, Christina Sinisi writes stories about families, the broken and blessed. Her published books include *The Christmas Confusion* and the upcoming *Sweet Summer*, as well as Christmas On Ocracoke. Married for 35 years, she is the mother of two wonderful grown children and lives in South Carolina.

A New Day

Glenda Durano

Sitting under the New Mexico sky, away from the glow of the city lights, I stare upward fascinated by the stars. It's amazing to think that even during the day, the stars are still shining in heaven; we just can't see them until it's dark.

Sometimes it's that way with God, too. As long as life is bright and cheery, we don't really see Him—because we aren't looking for Him. But when physical, emotional, or spiritual darkness comes, we seek Him desperately. Fortunately, Jeremiah 29:13 promises, *"You will seek me and find me when you seek me with all your heart"* (NIV). Many times, the more extreme our circumstances are, the more clearly we see Him. In other words, the darker the night is, the brighter the light.

Every room in my house has a light. Some fixtures, like those in my dining room, are grand and glorious, illuminating the entire room through a shade of shimmering crystals. Other lights, like the lamp on my desk, serve a more practical purpose, enabling me to see better so I can do my work more efficiently. The light for which I am most grateful, however, is not the most beautiful or the most efficient. My most beloved light is the tiny blue nightlight guiding me to my bathroom in the middle of the night. When life is the darkest—literally or figuratively—I need light the most.

Even as an adult, I was afraid of the dark. As far as I could tell, there was nothing good about the night: it was cold, hard, and unfriendly. One day, however, as I was reading Genesis 1, I noticed the wording God used to describe the completion of each day of creation: *"And there was evening and there was morning – the first day"* (Genesis 1:5 NIV).

In Jewish culture, the day begins with evening. As dusk transitions into night, the world grows dark, but then, just as night is at its darkest point, morning breaks into a new day. This mindset carries over to Western culture in our usage of the twelve-hour clock, with 12:00 a.m. (midnight) marking the beginning of a new day. Literally, a new beginning commences at the darkest time.

Spiritually, a new day means that God is stretching you – doing something fresh in you. Isaiah 43:19 (NIV) says, *"See, I am doing a new thing! Now it springs up; do you not perceive it? I am making a way in the wilderness and streams in the wasteland."* When you're in the dark and can't seem to find your way, it's easy to feel as if you're lost in the wilderness. You may not know where you are, but God does. And He's right there, too – encouraging you to draw near to Him, listen more carefully to Him, and not merely seek His ways, but seek Him.

When Jesus was in the wilderness (Matthew 4:1-11), He was tempted by Satan. It was a hard time and a dark time. Although Jesus knew everything, He still ended up in a cruel place of temptation. Why? Because, Matthew 4:1 (NIV) tells us, *"Jesus was led by the Spirit…"*

Although God is Light, He can use the darkness for His purposes. Sometimes, we have to be in the dark to see the Light more clearly. If you're at that point right now, take heart. When it seems as if life can't get any darker, a new day is on the way.

Glenda loves to encourage others. As a Certified Educational Planner, she has published three books about college planning from a Christian perspective. She's currently writing a narrative non-fiction book about how God used disability in her family to demonstrate His unconditional love.

Saul's Darkness

Rhonnie Cough

Blinded by power and fueled by rage, he walked the road to Damascus with a taste for blood and conquest on his mind. Saul planned to continue his rise in the ranks of the Jewish learned and purge from among them the followers of the Way. As he and his men approached the city, they prepared to turn more agitators into prisoners, blasphemers into examples.

Until a light from Heaven and the voice of Jesus brought him to his knees.

And the spiritual darkness he had been walking in became literal as his world was suddenly devoid of light. It was in this darkness that he would learn to finally see.

Jesus met Saul on the middle of his hatred, on the road to another bloody escapade. Even though Saul was the Chief of Sinners, Jesus called him by name.

If Jesus can reach down into the life of Saul, the great persecutor of the early Church, and transform him into the apostle Paul, what can He do with us?

In Psalm 139, we learn that God's presence is everywhere, reaching the highest heights and descending into the deepest depths. *"If I say, "Surely the darkness will hide me and the light will become night around me," even the darkness will not be dark to you; the night will shine like the day, for darkness is as light to you* (verses 11-12 NIV).

Darkness is nothing for Christ, who became sin for us. Jesus took Saul's darkness and inserted His Holy light. That light was enough to transform Saul's life and cause him to recognize in Romans 4:8 that the Son of God died for us while we were still sinners.

What darkness is keeping you from God's holy light? Remember that because of Jesus' work on the cross, our darkness is nothing to Him. It is in the depths of our sin that His light may shine brightest. Let's draw near to Him and allow Him to illuminate our lives. He is willing and able to bring us out of our darkness and into His wonderful light.

Rhonnie Cough was born in Charleston, South Carolina into a Navy family. After living in Florida and Hawaii, she spent most of her formative years in Northern California. She has been a student of God's Word for twenty years. She lives in South Carolina with her husband and two dogs.

Night Light

L. A. Robbins

The Cumberland Gap Pass through the Appalachian Mountains was secluded, yet beautiful. During the daylight hours the bright sun and colorful landscape evoked great joy to those who called this place home. The moonless nights often left Agnes's family encased in darkness.

    Agnes lay still beneath Grandma's homemade quilt and drifted to sleep. She was soon awoken as she heard her mother's angry voice yelling, "Look at this mess, you have wet the bed again. All I need is more sheets to wash." The belt whipped through the dark air and wrapped around Agnes's skinny little legs. She began to weep from the pain. "Shut up, we don't need to hear you crying. It is your own doing that brought this on", screamed Mommy. "Mommy please", whimpered Agnes, "I didn't mean to pee the bed." "I have heard that before. Get up, now", Mommy yelled as she swung the belt back ready to give another blow. Agnes meekly obeyed to avoid the sting of another lashing. She made her way to the shabby dresser in the dreary room. As she searched for a tattered gown and underwear to change into, tears began to run like a raging river. She kept her back to Mommy because she would beat her again if she saw her crying. "Agnes, hurry up, back to bed for you. You are more trouble than you are worth. I have had nothing but problems since you came into this world." Mommy stated flatly. Agnes felt a rush of despair fill her tiny frame until she remembered, tomorrow she was going to spend a week with grandpa, or dad as she called him. Her soul felt hope.

Agnes trudged through the dark night as fast as her scrawny legs could carry her. Dad walked beside her, his silhouette looming large above her as she tried to stay close. The night sounds of the country road were of no comfort to Agnes as she followed Dad. She held the coal oil lantern tightly in her hands. She could not afford to drop it and put out the only light she had. Her heart pounded, fearing the darkness if she dropped the lantern. Dad took the lantern when he sensed Agnes was unable to hold it still for both of them. He rested his free hand upon her shoulder and explained to her that sharing a light was inadequate and that it would be better if they each had their own light.

"Agnes," Dad said, "It is impossible to walk in someone else's light. Next time we will bring you a smaller lantern and you can use your own light to lead you through the night." This memory with Dad proved to shed light on a true teaching that would last a lifetime.

Agnes, now fifteen, had survived a harsh upbringing. Life had been hard after the biological father she had never known had been taken too early by the hands of an angry man. She had been protected from the pain in her mother's womb at the time, but her first fifteen years had proven to bear marks of the murder. Nervous nights of beatings from her overwhelmed mother, who somehow associated the killing of her father during her pregnancy to Agnes, had been traumatic. She was now convinced that she would never amount to anything as childhood trauma had scared her within. Sometimes Agnes felt hopeless.

As Agnes sat in the small country church, she sensed a glorious light nudging at her heart. This excited and troubled her at the same time. She contemplated this stirring within throughout the night and the next day. She would go back and respond willingly to the voice that invited her to walk in the light. Agnes responded and the author of the light accepted her willing heart. She was forever changed. Peace like she had never known flooded her body and her spirit felt light. She was delivered from her heavy load. In spite of the past Agnes now felt more hopeful.

One dewy morning, a few days later, Agnes knelt in the grass just outside the shack that housed her single mom, herself, and her brothers. The calm crisp morning held a moment she would never forget. The presence of the new light wrapped her up in a shroud of comfort that was electrifying. Never had she felt such a powerful manifestation that brought a peace beyond understanding and a joy that could not be spoken. All her dark days seemed a distant memory as she bowed her youthful heart and body and became captivated in the eternal light that had ignited her soul.

Agnes met Wayne and quickly fell in love so she quit school and married him at age seventeen. Dropping out of school to marry and start a family was acceptable in the fifties, in her Southern rural community. Agnes spent thirty-five years married to an unbeliever. She worked at her unequally yoked marriage with diligence. She pleased him the best she could but they did not always share the same understanding of life. He was a bit rough around the edges as his Southern raising had instilled and she was a strong willed fighter for her family and friends. Baby number one came and Agnes was resolute to provide more security and stability than she had been given. She was sure to nurture and give love in order to shelter her family from pain. A baby boy was also soon added to Agnes' little family. With new responsibility came more resolution to pursue and conquer the pain of the pain. Passing on the curse was unacceptable. With this pursuit Agnes experienced perplexing odds as she strived to carry the light for her husband, her children, her church family and her friends. Surely she could hold the light that others needed so that they might walk in darkness without experiencing the pain and heartache that she had.

Without the light that she had received so long ago she would have fallen into utter emotional and spiritual darkness. Daily devotion to her instruction book and prayer time kept the flame burning and hope alive. Agnes was unable to hold the light for those she loved the most but she pressed onward. She would pray that they too would receive the glorious light that had led her throughout the years. Her life had always been challenging, even in the womb, but she could not give into the anxiety, the doubts and the fears that warred against her. She must walk in the light that she has been given in order to expel the reverberating darkness.

Wayne was dying. Eight years of the eroding disease had left his body weary. Trips, treatments and turmoil had ensued as they took every avenue possible to save his life. Agnes sat by her husband's bedside and loved him unconditionally. She comforted him, bathed him, and nurtured his wounds. The tracheotomy was permanent as the cancer had eaten away the tissue in his throat. His voice was nearly inaudible from the vocal cord damage yet he whispered, "Agnes you have been a good wife, you have done better than you thought." She would carry that comment to her grave. As Wayne began to hemorrhage, the sight was more than Agnes could bear. "Please dear God," she prayed, "the suffering must soon be over, for this is more than we can bear." Her prayers were answered and Wayne entered into eternal glory. He too had received the light just a few years prior.

Battles had been fought, some lost and some won, but the war was almost over. Now eighty-eight, Agnes lay in bed unable to do for others as she had in the past. Her life seemed useless now because she was accustomed to serving others diligently. Acceptance was inevitable. Her life was fading but yet the light of her Savior was still burning within. Her flame had flickered and at times grown dim but nothing had been able to put out her light. Agnes had her own light. She had not walked through this dark world in the light of others but she had carried a lantern that had been fueled with eternal oil from above. Agnes soon slipped into eternal rest and has now entered into the presence of her light giver where there will never be night. Eternal light shines in glory; no night light is needed.

"And there shall be no night there; and they need no candle, neither light of the sun; for the Lord God giveth them light: and they shall reign for ever and ever" (Rev. 22:5, KJV).

L.A. Robbins is an aspiring author who feels called to write with a purpose to encourage women and children. She lives in rural Tennessee with her husband. She is a mother of three adult children and Nana to two sweet granddaughters.

Dark Night

Sandra Vosburgh

The night felt dark—that is, if dark can be felt. Yet, I knew it could.

I paced behind my Camaro and waited for the service truck, my hands shoved deep in the pockets of my jeans. Tears ran down my face, and I let them. The hoot of an owl stopped my pacing—I took a deep breath, then continued to wear a path in the grass.

The mild rumble of a vehicle grew until headlights shot lasers into the sky. Then I saw the van pop over the top of the hill. The driver slowed and stopped near me on the shoulder of the road. A burly man left the cab and trudged toward me. "You know what time it is?" he said, through clenched teeth. "Three o'clock."

"Yes, sir. I'm sorry."

Stan—according to the name on his jacket—mumbled something and glared at my flat tire. "New cars don't come with jacks and spares, anymore?"

I lowered my head. What could I say, 'Probably, but I've never changed a tire? That my dad never took the time to show me?'

He rubbed the stubble on his chin as he scanned the road that wound through the back hills, thirty miles from the nearest town. "Top of a hill, on a curve." He shook his head. "Not the smartest place to pull off."

"Yes, sir. I'm sorry."

I followed him as he moved to my driver's door and opened it. He plunked down on the seat and yanked on the emergency brake release with a glance at the passenger seat.

I froze. *My dad's gun.* My heart banged against the walls of my brain. Sweat formed above my lips as I licked and chewed them.

Stan started my car, and again I followed. He drove a few yards and parked my Camaro further off the road. He then picked up the pistol and removed the bullets. He lay the gun down and put the bullets in his jacket pocket.

His eyes grazed mine as he got out.

Stan went to work changing the flat, and I went back to shuffling, sniffling, and shoving back the impulse to sob. I watched him. Who else would show me how to change a tire?

In silence, like his mind was preoccupied, Stan moved mechanically until the moment he let down the jack and tightened the bolts. He put away his tools, then moved to stand beside me while wiping his hands on a rag.

His hands looked rough and dry, and I doubted Stan had ever lived anything like my dad, holed up in an office, oblivious to—

"Son," Stan pulled me back, "what are you doing here? Alone. In the middle of the night?"

"I . . . just wanted to clear my head," I said, feeling shame.

He ran a hand through his graying hair. "I know what you're doing."

My eyes darted to his. They were moist.

"I won't take the gun," Stan said, "but I will take the bullets. Is that all right?" He placed a hand on my shoulder; it felt weighted like he needed me to pay attention.

I could barely breathe. "Yes, sir."

"I'm going to pray with you."

Tears flooded my eyes. I couldn't hold them back.

"Then we're going to call your mother. Is that all right?"

"Yes, sir."

This young man invited light when he placed the call to one who could help him. When exposed, his desperation was met with compassion. He then humbly submitted to the knight's guidance, turning first to God in prayer, then returning home. He did not hear the hovering whispers of God that night, saying, "Let there be light." Yet, it was so.

Sandra Vosburgh is a pastor's wife, women's ministry director, Bible teacher, and author of A Deadly Sin Mystery series. The mother of five and grandmother of fifteen, Sandra is also the winner of the 2021 Carolina Christian Writers Conference award in fiction.

Having Faith with Chronic Illness

Taryn Dryfhout

Health is something that we don't think about until we don't have it. I've had a decade to reflect on what it means to trust in God's word amidst my struggles and have come to realize that God uses all circumstances to reveal himself.

My adult life has been a turbulent battle to stay healthy. I spend between two and six weeks as an in-patient in a hospital every year, and one day each week as an outpatient. I take more than a dozen pills each day as well as a series of injections, and I live with chronic pain. I also struggle with fatigue, dizziness, migraines and many other symptoms which make life difficult and limits what I can achieve each day.

Naturally, managing several chronic health conditions takes a toll on your emotions. As a result of some of my experiences, I suffer from Post-Traumatic Stress Disorder and anxiety, both of which manifest more severely when I am unwell. Poor health also takes an emotional toll on those around you, and has changed our family. My husband no longer works, so that he can care for the children while I attend health appointments, am admitted to the hospital or I'm simply unwell at home. He has become a calming, consoling presence in my life, helping me navigate the emotional rollercoaster that I am on as a result of my ongoing health issues. He is also burdened with the emotions that come with all of that. Because of the unpredictable nature of my health, my oldest child has also developed anxiety. More than once he has awakened, only to find that Mummy went away in an ambulance overnight. He has even witnessed emergency services attending to me. My mother has also been burdened with my health problems, often coming with me to appointments and enduring many of my emotional meltdowns. She has been with me during invasive procedures and stood beside me in an operating theatre when the situation looked very bleak. Being sick challenges not only myself, but everyone around me — it is a struggle that we have come to experience as a family.

James 1:2-3 says, *"Consider it pure joy, my brothers and sisters, whenever you face trials of many kinds, because you know that the testing of your faith produces perseverance"* (NIV).

You have heard the saying 'Every cloud has a silver lining,' and many scriptures attest to this. God can use every experience, including suffering, to help us think more deeply about Him, and about our life and its meaning. I have changed dramatically from when I was a healthy young woman. Experiencing trials has helped me to rely on God and seek comfort from Him, deepening my trust and relationship with Him. Any experience which results in suffering pushes us to experience spiritual growth, because we look to our Father as He works in and through us, and as He breathes meaning into every experience.

God can use any experience for His glory. That doesn't mean that God has chosen for me to be unwell or that He enjoys it. Rather, God can take things and turn them into something that is good and which reveals and glorifies Him. God may use our circumstances to help us grow in our faith and character, or He may use our experience to shape us into servants who can minister to others who are suffering. Despite the limits that my health has put on me, God has blessed my family in ways that I could never have imagined ten years ago. He has led us to raise a large family, opened up a way for me to work from home, and this has allowed me to study what I love. These things haven't been without their difficulties, but God has come through and shown me that *"I can do all things, through Christ who strengthens me"* (Philippians 4:13 NIV).

I don't have full control of my life, and that brings me great comfort. I often joke with my family that I am passive in my own life, waiting patiently to see what God has in store for me next, but in truth, it brings me great peace to know that God is in control. Psalm 31:15 says *"My times are in your hands"* (NIV). God controls all things even when it may seem like things, such as my health, are careening out of control. Our times belong to God, so I continue to lift up my health to Him, who is in control of all things.

I continue to pray for healing, knowing that God hears my prayers, and trust that He is with me always, through my physical struggles. I have had some very serious situations with my health over the last few years and have come to realize that God has already kept me from circumstances much worse. I am grateful for the healing presence that God has had, and continues to have in my life. Psalm 146:2 (NIV) sums it up perfectly:

"I will praise the LORD as long as I live. I will sing praises to my God with my dying breath."

Taryn is a New Zealand writer whose publication record includes non-fiction books, college courses, website content, and more than 400 feature articles, reviews, and columns published in newspapers, websites, and magazines. Taryn is a full member of the New Zealand Society of Authors (NZSA), and New Zealand Christian Writers (NZCW).

Sally and Buster

Cheryl D. Coffman

Today was the last day. We had been putting this off for weeks and the time had arrived. Sally had lived on this 19th century demonstration farm for more years than any employee could remember. It just felt like she's always been here watching over the various sheep and goats that had come and gone on this farm.

This day the manager was out sick, so I was chosen to take Sally, the Australian shepherd who faithfully herded the flock, to her final veterinarian visit. I am just another human to Sally. With the sheep, that is another story. She knows each one by name. I can call a particular one and she would run right to that sheep and herd it home to the pen. She demonstrated this ability to many school children who visited the farm while on field trips. She amazed us with her intelligence and agility. She knew exactly what time the sheep would be let out of the pen. No matter which employee was working that day, when they arrived to the pen, Sally would be waiting at the gate rain, or snow.

Our veterinarian told us that Sally must be some kind of Australian shepherd mix, more from her behaviors and intelligence than her looks. Sally was solid black and had light brown eyes almost golden in the daylight. Several years ago, one of the employees trained her to bring the cows up to the barn. She reluctantly did her daily chore each evening. Cows were below her calling in life. As soon as they got close to the barn, she would take off trotting back to her sheep to bring her flock into their fold.

She was special to the employees on this farm. When her animals were up for the night she would find a place to sleep in the horse barn. It was an interesting place to sleep because she was skittish around the mules and horses. Sally never bothered the geese on the farm. We surmised that perhaps years before, she had been pecked enough to make her keep her distance. On the original farm the geese, ducks, and chickens would roam free during the day, and keep the bugs out of the gardens. One story we tell is how the farm children always carried a stout stick with them to beat the geese away or snakes.

A month ago, Sally tripped and fell while herding the sheep. She limped for days and would not even try to herd. Our veterinarian took ex-rays and said, "No broken bone or displaced hip but, (I hate it when any doctor uses the word 'but', it always spells trouble), Sally has a tumor on her hip next to the spine and it's growing. She is in pain and will need to be euthanized soon."

We were in shock and could hardly believe that Sally would no longer be on the farm. The manager decided that this was the date. How unlucky for me to be chosen to take her the twenty miles to town and the vet. I would not be wearing my costume and bonnet, but hoping she would recognize my voice. I was driving the company truck with Sally sitting up front as friendly and alert as always. She slowly laid down and put her head on my lap.

"Oh Sally this is not good for my heart. I am the one taking you to your demise and now you are loving on me."

* * * *

While we were sitting in the waiting room a man and his son entered dragging a Great Pyrenees. Neither father nor son looked happy. Maybe they were here for the same reason. Sally and I sat across the room dejected.

I said. "Beautiful dog you have. Is it a pure Pyrenees? They are good with sheep." The father said. "That is what they say but a house pet he is not. We are the third family that he has had, and he is still as wild as a buck."

"That is a shame."

The boy said. "No, the shame is that he has torn up every lawn chair, bush and flower bed and hose, we have in our yard. He chews shoes and umbrellas. You name it, he can destroy it quickly. Our cousins that had him before us, said they had to replace their swimming pool liner that cost thousands of dollars because of him."

"He sounds like a handful for sure. What is he here for today?"

The father said, "We are getting rid of him. No one wants him."

"Really? Have you tried to give him away?"

They both laughed, and then the father said, "Everyone we know in Henry County has seen and read all about the dirty tricks he has pulled when my daughter posted them on social media. So, when I posted that I would give the dog away to a suitable home my phone went silent. One friend texted me and said, 'Good Luck'."

The assistant called for Sally. I gave her one last hug from all of us at the farm and took another photo. I stood up and saluted her good-bye as they walked her limping into the back room.

I remained there. I could not walk out that door. I had the crazy notion of asking the man for his dog. I had not talked with the manager about another dog. No one has even suggested that we replace Sally. What would they say if I brought a troublesome dog on the farm? What would the insurance company do if a visitor or employee got bit. Before I knew it, out of my mouth came the words that I would regret for a long time.

"Would you be willing to donate him to the 1850 Smithfield Family Farm?"

The son jumped up, "For sure. When? Today, I hope? I'll pay you money to take him."

"Well as you just saw we are saying goodbye to our sheep dog who has cancer. Do you have papers on him? What is his name?

"We are not sure who was the first owner. A vet sometime in the past had him fixed trying to calm him down. It did not work. We have his shot records for the past three years."

The son added. "We call him Buster because he busted everything. I guess he has had different names in the past."

I walked over to him and let him smell me and Sally on my clothes. He did not pay attention, no growl, no adverse reactions to the smell of another dog.

"Is he usually this calm with strangers."

The father laughed. "Yes, he ignores them, unless they try and hold him down. Then he will growl. We have never had him bite anyone but we have only had him for eight months. We can't afford his destructive habits. He dug under the fence and tore up my neighbor's flower beds. We had to replace them this week. That was the last straw for us."

I thought to call the company manager and then I paused, knowing she would say no. She always says no. She thinks that an idea from an employee, even a cost saving idea, is ridiculous. All good ideas have to come down from the board of directors.

I was shocked when out of my mouth came these words. "I want to try him on our farm. Hopefully he will calm down and behave when he has a job with sheep. Do you know if he has been around sheep or cattle?

The son said, "He is five years old and no one has mentioned that he came from a farm."

The assistant then appeared and said. "Miss Connor you can pull the truck around back."

"If you choose to donate him, give me those papers and follow me to the farm. We will go in the back gate and you can let him off there. Don't tell your daughter where you donated him or he will be back in your front yard the next day. And I will be looking for a new job."

* * * *

At the farm, I took his leash, looked into that shaggy face and smiled, "Buster your new life begins today as a farm dog. You are blessed by God to have once been lost, and now found to your true calling in life."

We walked out to the sheep pen. He sniffed around, sat down on the dry hay, and watched me prepare his food.

The next morning the staff along with Buster gathered in the sheep pasture to pay our tributes and place a wooden cross over Sally's grave. "RIP Sally, 2015, Boundless devotion to her sheep."

Cheryl Coffman is a writer of Christian fiction. She writes short stories and novels. She hopes you enjoy this animal story of kindness and grace.

The Light Diffuses

Melody M. Morrison

In the wee hours of morning, one of the nurses confronted me rather harshly, "How can you be so calm? Don't you know he might die?" These are the shocking words this mother heard from a registered nurse, the mother-in-law of a friend, on that intense, blustery night in the children's hospital ward.

Until this night, life had been good to us. I had finished my college education in three years acquiring a music teacher's position. Four days after graduation, I married my high school sweet heart after four years of dating, attending church, and leading youth group together. About three years into the marriage, we experienced the joyous birth of our precious baby boy, Benjamin. We were ecstatic. Two years later, a beautiful baby girl, Jessica, was born. Less than a year later, our little family encountered our first major emergency.

Weather had snapped from a lovely spring morning to a damp, windy, chilly afternoon as March delivers. Later that night, Benjamin developed a cold with fever and soon became somewhat lethargic. By phone, I explained this to our seasoned, laid-back pediatrician and remarked that Ben's eyes 'just didn't look right'. Without hesitation, he said to bundle him up well and meet him at the hospital ER immediately. In a short time, the doctor told me Benjamin had developed a severe pneumonia in both lungs and he must be admitted. I knew as I carried him to the dark, sterile hospital room, head lying limply on my shoulder, he was quite ill. I was not about to leave him except when my husband would bring Jessica to nurse. I did what I could to comfort him. He reached for me, but Benjamin was under an oxygen tent so I couldn't even hold this fragile little boy's body close to me. The fear and confusion shone in his eyes, so I just loved him with words - reading, talking and singing to him gently.

I was shocked by the nurse's question but all I could think to say was, "Well, he's in bigger hands than mine." The answer just came out. I said what I thought I *should* say, I suppose.

All night I hovered close to Benjamin. I pondered the nurse's comment and my response. Should I be more upset? Why wasn't I? Was there something deeply wrong with me? Through our room's window, dawn began to bring brilliant colors to a new day, beckoning me to talk openly with God. I told him I thought I must be overwhelmed or numb, yet I somehow felt peaceful, in deep love for that little person lying helpless. But I knew he belonged to God before I had ever seen him the first time.

As I thanked God for Benjamin in the quiet, I accepted that a powerful peace had undergirded me from the moment I noticed his dazed eyes and shallow breathing. Those first twenty-five years I had been spent learning about God's power and love from His Word and His music had prepared me. Life had been relatively easy and uncomplicated until this event. At that moment of recognition of the *source* of my peace, the sunlight burst through the clouds on the horizon and I was washed with rays of warmth like I had never experienced. Suddenly scriptures from my years in my church girls' group flooded through my mind. *"What time I am afraid, I will trust in thee"* Psalm 56:3 KJV. *"And lo, I am with you always..."* Matthew 28:20 KJV. *"Trust in the Lord always and lean not unto thine own understanding. In all thy ways acknowledge him and he will direct thy paths"* Proverbs 3:5-6 KJV. What assurance! Unknowingly, I had banked deep faith for the crisis. I knew in theory that God is omnipresent. Now I knew this truth by absolute experience. The Father of Light proved His Word true in the light of a multi-color sunrise.

I looked across to my little boy, still breathing shallowly, but awake and smiling. Seeing the sunlight reflect in his eyes, I knew he felt it, too. I couldn't help but sing our song, "God is so good to Benjamin. God is so good to Jessica. God is so good to mom and dad, so good to me."

Melody enjoys being wife, mother, gramma, musician, teacher, writer and world traveler. Her greatest passion is to use her artistic endeavors to celebrate and bring about recognition of the immeasurable value of all people as unique treasures of the Creator and to encourage their dynamic transformation available through Christ's love.

One More Little One

Adria Wilkins

"Neither do people light a lamp and put it under a bowl. Instead they put it on its stand, and it gives light to everyone in the house" (Matthew 5:15 NIV).

Maggie was fidgeting in her seat across from me at a restaurant, her eyes strained with tension. Her fifteen-year-old daughter Sarah was pregnant, she told me, and planning to have an abortion.

My soul was crushed, and my heartbeat quickened. I wanted to help this family and stop this tragedy from happening, but I had no idea where to begin.

I had met Maggie, a down-to-earth lady in her late 30s, as part of my side business selling candles in homes. Maggie had hosted a party to receive some free products, and we were meeting at the restaurant to finalize the orders.

I never made any money selling candles, because I bought candles for myself with the profit. Often, I wondered why I bothered to lug the products to people's houses, give sales pitches, and then drag myself home, exhausted.

While sitting with Maggie, I asked some questions about their home life. Maggie was a single mom. Her finances were tight, and she didn't know how they could possibly feed another child.

As I left the restaurant my heart was heavy. I felt an urgency that something had to be done.

I remembered a lady at our church, Kathy, had volunteered for a hotline that counseled women with unplanned pregnancies. It was late when I got home, but I called Kathy just after I walked in the door.

Kathy immediately calmed my spirits. She asked me how to reach Sarah and I gave her the family's number.

"Let's say a prayer together," she said. "When I feel God's prompting, I will call, and we'll pray that Sarah answers."

Several days later, Kathy called me. "You won't believe this. I called the family's house last night and I heard a little, timid voice answer the phone."

"Is this Sarah?" Kathy had asked.

"Yes."

"You don't know me, but I'm calling to encourage you not to have an abortion. There is a baby inside you that has fingers, toes and a heart."

Kathy began to hear sniffles on the other end of the line. She knew all the right words to say to prick Sarah's heart.

The next day, Sarah's mom called me to finalize the candle order. "You won't believe this, but Sarah told me this morning she's changed her mind and is going to have the baby," she said, her voice laced with hope.

Maggie was thrilled. I was thrilled. As soon as I got off the phone, I called Kathy to tell her the news. We had witnessed God turn a bleak situation into a joyous occasion.

At that very moment, I knew why God had me in the candle business.

Maggie's candle order arrived two weeks later, and we met again at the same restaurant. In walked Sarah, who was wearing a baby bump and pregnancy glow. I hugged both of them, trying to sound encouraging without giving away my secret.

The family was still having financial trouble. My heart was burdened for them. As I drove home that night, I had an idea. Maybe the women's mission group at my church could throw a baby shower for Sarah. The group of 10-15 ladies were often caring for needy families with a food pantry and a clothes closet. I called Kathy and she was on board. I contacted Maggie. She talked with Sarah and they were both very touched by the idea, accepting our offer with few words.

"What kinds of things do y'all need?" I asked.

"Everything!" Maggie said.

Several weeks later, Sarah and her mom drove to our church. The shower was held in the parlor room, which was decorated with wrapped gifts. Sarah and Maggie sat up front, wearing corsages we had brought. Sarah opened packages filled with diapers, clothes, a stroller and a crib. After many thanks and hugs, the family drove away with their car packed to the ceiling.

Sarah didn't know that her mysterious caller had been sitting in that parlor room. Throughout the shower, I kept glancing over at Kathy, who wore an indescribable grin that seemed to cover her whole body.

When I hear the song, "This little light of mine, I'm gonna let it shine." I think about Sarah, Maggie and the baby that was born.

Who would have thought candles could save a little one?

Award winning author, Adria Wilkins has an accounting degree from Western Kentucky University. Her book "The Joy Box Journal" with Hachette Book Group released July 2019. After suffering the unthinkable - death of three-year-old Blake, she found that Jesus sustains, and even surprises His followers with joy.

Tears at a Church Meeting

Melissa Henderson

With papers collected in my red folder for the Missions team, I found my usual seat next to the folding table. Waiting patiently in the fellowship hall at church, I prepared to give a report for my group. People exchanged greetings as they entered the room and found their seats. The meeting opened with prayer and the conversation began.

A usual monthly meeting gave the opportunity for each leader to share updates on their team activities. Discussions included budget concerns, mission trip possibilities, prayer requests, and upcoming projects.

I was pleased to have a detailed report to share with everyone.

Each team representative listened and asked questions of the person presenting. A productive meeting.

My turn to speak about the Mission team was coming. Checking my list and notes, I cleared my throat and prepared to speak.

The telephone in the church kitchen began ringing. Thinking the sound would soon stop and whoever was calling would leave a message, we continued the discussion.

The phone continued to ring. Each person looked up from their papers and glanced toward the kitchen. Another attendee rose and headed to answer the call. I looked toward the man as he spoke and I heard my name mentioned.

Phone put on hold while my friend came to the table. He walked next to me, placed his hand on my shoulder and spoke in a quiet voice.

"Melissa, you have a phone call. There is an emergency with your son. Your husband is waiting to talk with you."

I gasped. "What? Do you know what has happened?" Asking the questions while bolting from my seat to race to the phone, I didn't wait for his answer.

Grabbing the kitchen phone, I spoke. "Hello. What's wrong? What happened?" I was out of breath.

My husband Alan shared how he had received a phone call from our young adult son. Mike was at the hospital. He had gone to the doctor about a rash and fatigue. The doctor told him to go to the emergency room immediately.

"I'll be right there to get you. We'll head to the hospital." Alan was already leaving home.

"I'll be at the front door of the church. Hurry." I tried not to cry.

Walking back into the fellowship hall, I explained to my friends that our son was in the hospital. I didn't have details, but there was an issue with his blood work.

My dear friends paused the meeting to gather in prayer. I listened to the words, thanked the group, gathered my belongings, and raced to the front door of the church.

Alan arrived within minutes, yet time seemed to stand still.

"What's going on? Where is he? Is Mike hurt?"

"Melissa, he's in the hospital and the doctors are running tests. His blood platelets are low." Alan and I prayed as we rode to the local hospital. Arriving, we found our way to Mike's room. Seeing our young adult son in a bed, wearing a hospital gown, and hooked up to IVs, more tears began to fall from my eyes.

Hugging Mike softly, I asked questions and hoped for answers. The blood work results were not conclusive. The waiting period began.

The black of the night made the darkness of the unknown medical condition more troublesome. We wanted answers now. More tears.

Mike was not in pain. He was fatigued and didn't want to spend time in the hospital. More frustrated than sick. He wanted answers, too.

Prayers. Tears. Feeling breathless and desperate. Darkness. Fear of the unknown.

Until . . . we turned everything over to God. Asking God to heal our son and to bring peace and comfort to his body. Asking God to guide the medical professionals to find the correct answers for the mysterious rash and fatigue.

And then, there was light . . .

The next morning, testing revealed answers. A blood disorder called ITP was causing low blood platelet count which created petechiae, a pinpoint looking rash. The disorder caused his extreme fatigue, too.

Doctors administered medicines. Mike stayed in the hospital for days, being monitored as he healed.

Upon being discharged, he received instructions for handling his illness. No cause for the disorder was ever discovered. His hospital stay happened years ago. He is a healthy man with no recent recurrences of the condition. Praise the Lord!

In dark times, when we feel hopeless and afraid, we can go to God and find His light.

"The Lord is my light and my salvation – whom shall I fear? The Lord is the stronghold of my life – of whom shall I be afraid" (Psalm 27:1 NIV)?

Amen.

Award winning author Melissa Henderson writes inspirational messages laced with humor. With stories in books, magazines, and devotionals, Melissa encourages readers. Her passions are helping in community and church. Melissa is an Elder, Deacon and Stephen Minister. Follow Melissa on Facebook, Twitter, Pinterest and at http://www.melissaghenderson.com

True Light Shines

Tammy Hill

How easy to sense the presence of God as sun is shining down.

Rays kiss your face, that warm embrace, a peace at last is found.

But clouds grow dark, sunlight fades, and brightness all goes dim.

His presence still surrounds you. Put your trust in Him.

Emotions birth inconsistencies in where to find relief.

Your loving Father won't leave your side in happiness or grief.

Trust His truth for you and me, His promises reveal:

Precious to Him, we all are seen and certain is His will.

"Again, a new commandment I write to you, which thing is true in Him and in you, because the darkness is passing away, and the true light is already shining."
(1 John 2:8 NKJV)

A step of faith led Tammy Hill to a Bible study, unlocking the value of studying God's word and prompting her to share that joy. As a women's ministry leader, she has the privilege of mentoring, supporting, and encouraging others in their walk with Christ.

Image Interior Images

Used by Permission

Page 6, Candle, www.clker.com, by Ocal 11-18-07

Page 16, Flashlights, www.clipartstation.com, Maribel Rosa, artist

Page 26, Light Bulb, www.openclipart.org

Page 36, Lantern, www.openclipart.org

Page 50, Lighthouse, www.Cliparts.zone

Living Parables of Central Florida, Inc., of which EABooks Publishing is a division, supports Christian charities providing for the needs of their communities. Ministries are encouraged to join hands and hearts with like-minded charities to better meet unmet needs in their communities. Annually the Board of Directors chooses the recipients of seed money to facilitate the beginning stages of these charitable activities.

Mission Statement

To empower start up, nonprofit organizations financially, spiritually, and with sound business knowledge to participate successfully as a responsible 501(c)3 organization that contributes to the Kingdom work of God.

GPS Grant Program

The goal of the GPS Program: The GPS (God's Positioning System) provides a solid foundation for running a successful non-profit through a year-long coaching process and a grant for start-up needs, eventually allowing these charities to successfully apply for grants and loans from others so they can further meet unmet needs in their communities.

www.ingramcontent.com/pod-product-compliance
Lightning Source LLC
Chambersburg PA
CBHW071746040426
42446CB00012B/2479